THOUGHTS

FOR THE

CHRISTIAN LAITY.

BY THE

REV. H. PADDON, M.A.,

OF TRINITY COLLEGE, OXFORD, AND LATE VICAR OF HIGH WYCOMBE, BUCKS.
AUTHOR OF ' THOUGHTS ON THE EVANGELICAL PREACHING OF THE
PRESENT DAY," ETC., ETC.

"A wonderful and horrible thing s committed in the land; the prophets
prophesy falsely . . . . . and my people love to have it so. And
what will ye do in the end thereof?" —JER. v. 30, 31.

SECOND EDITION.

LONDON:
WILLIAM MACINTOSH, 24, PATERNOSTER ROW.
1873.

FOURPENCE EACH, 3s. 6d. a Dozen, £1 5s. a Hundred.
May be had direct from the Author, if preferred, on application by Post, at Sussex
Gardens, Eastbourne.

PREFACE TO SECOND EDITION.

———◆———

Soon after the appearance of my Address to my Brethren the Evangelical Clergy, on the Preaching of the Present Day, I was requested to consider whether it might not be the Lord's will that I should address the Christian Laity. The idea was not new to me, for I had introduced into my former Pamphlet a few thoughts for the consideration of my Lay Brethren, but struck them out lest they should divert the minds of my readers from the main object with which it was written.

I now offer my thoughts concerning themselves and their responsibility at this solemn crisis, to the Christian Laity. What may be their reception of this humble effort, I know not, but *this* I know, that every word is written in *love*, and every thought is steeped in *prayer*. To God's blessing I would commend both my Pamphlet and my readers.

Need I add, let the present awful crisis be a time of *unceasing prayer* with the Christian Laity. God's promise is, "Prove Me now if I will not open the windows of "heaven and pour you out a blessing that there shall not "be room enough to hold it." And, again, "I will give "you *showers* of blessings." The words of Asa should often be on our lips, "Lord, it is nothing with Thee to help, "whether with many, or with them that have no power. "Help us, O Lord our God, for we rest on Thee, and in Thy "Name we go against this great multitude. O Lord, Thou "art our God; let not mortal man prevail against us."

THE AUTHOR.

Sussex Gardens, Eastbourne,
    April, 1873.

THOUGHTS

FOR THE

Christian Laity of the Present Day.

———

In a former Pamphlet I ventured to address my Brethren
in the Ministry upon "the Evangelical Preaching of the
"Present Day;" and although that Pamphlet has been very
heartily welcomed by many of the most devoted and faithful
servants of the Lord, the Clergy, *as a rule*, have resented it.
I am told that I might have expected this. Perhaps so.
Nevertheless I do heartily bless and praise the Lord for
having put it into my heart to write what I did. After
six months of reflection, during which six Editions have
been called for by the public, I can only see increasing cause
for deepest thankfulness that I was led to publish that
Pamphlet.

Before speaking to the Christian Laity in this Companion
Pamphlet, I will briefly quote a few passages from com-
munications which have reached me from Christian Editors
and others, and which confirm me in this feeling.

The Editor of the *Rock* writes :—" We have before us a
"treatise which we are glad to see has reached 'a fourth
"edition,' entitled, 'Thoughts on the Evangelical Preaching
"of the Present Day,' by the Rev. H. Paddon, M.A., late of
"Trinity College, Oxford, and late Vicar of High Wycombe,
"Bucks. (London : W. Mackintosh.) This treatise is in
"many ways suggestive, and deals with a subject of super-
"lative interest and importance. . . . . There is very
"much in the excellent treatise before us worthy of being

" studied, although the complaints are rather too sweeping.
" Our Author is intensely in earnest, and we trust his
" appeals will receive a still wider circulation; and, so far
" as applicable, be accompanied by a signal blessing from on
" high. All who desire the stability of the Church and the
" extension of the Redeemer's Kingdom may well study this
" treatise."

The Editor of the *Christian Standard* says :—" We rejoice
" to think that, notwithstanding the fearful errors which
" abound in the Church of England, and the lamentable luke-
" warmness which exists on the part of multitudes of the
" Evangelical Clergy, there are hundreds who share the feelings
" and cherish the sentiments of Mr. Paddon. And if they
" would only follow his example in raising, through means of
" the Press, a warning voice against the deadly errors and
" deplorable coldness of the day with the same earnestness
" and fidelity as he has done, we should see a marvellous
" revival of real religion not only in the Church of England,
" but throughout the realm of that Evangelicalism which
" at present is only no better than a mere name."

The same Editor writes :—" We shall have hereafter more
" occasions than one to recur to Mr. Paddon's Pamphlet.
" It is more than a confirmation of all that we have said in
" our various papers on ' The Preaching of the Present Day.'
" It could not have appeared more opportunely. It was
" much needed. It is written in a spirit of Christian
" courtesy, mingled with truthfulness and fidelity, which
" must give weight to truths which are of themselves of the
" most weighty kind."

A beloved Brother in the Lord writes :—" I believe
" in my very heart that you have done perfectly right
" in publishing your views upon that subject, which,
" to my mind, had remained untouched long enough. I

"fully believe with yourself that it is a very rare thing to "find the truth faithfully preached in the Establishment. "The preachers themselves think they do preach it in its "purity, but for the most part it is to be feared their eyes "are sadly blinded. How fearful will be the fate of false "teachers! . . . May your little work have the desired "effect. May the blessing of God attend it. May the "arrow of the Lord go forth like lightning with the book. " . . . . It will expose you to many buffetings "from men and devils, but not from God. I like " straightforward dealing, and truth demands it, and God " will bless it."

Another Brother says :—"I have read with deepest "interest your ' Thoughts,' and I feel greatly comforted and "strengthened by them. They have no uncertain sound, "and I earnestly trust that it will please God greatly to "bless them to their readers. . . . Death, or where "there is life, sleep reigns to a terrible extent so far as I " have seen."

An experienced and learned brother clergyman writes :— "I think you well describe the danger of the present "times. I am afraid the desire to please the professing "world has shaped the creed of many, so as to rub "off the salient points of the Gospel; and Ministers are too "apt to keep in the background what they know is un- "palatable to carnal reason or to carnal appetite. . . . "I don't suppose the English Church will hold long together, "being a house divided against itself. Worldly interests are "the *summum bonum* with many professors."

I must add yet the solemn words of one other much esteemed brother clergyman :—"I have seen," he says,"many, " by little and little giving up almost everything decidedly " and distinctively *evangelical;* until at length the services in

" their churches, the tunes, the decorations, the ever-changing
" and unauthorised customs, have come to savour more of
" the æsthetic ceremonial of Rome than of the simplicity
" of the Gospel of Christ. The trumpet gives an uncertain
" sound. The clear Gospel ring is wanting. . . . What
" marvel that the more spiritually-minded of the people
" should seek other pastures. The soul that has tasted the
" Bread of God cannot be satisfied with the husks of man's
" invention."

I might multiply witnesses to the need of some such
alarm as that which I ventured to sound, and which, as I have
said, my Brother Clergymen, as a rule, have resented, and
some of them, I grieve to say, very bitterly. Why, if the cap
does not fit, should any of us Evangelical Clergymen put it
on ? Such *over-sensitiveness* seems to my own mind to argue
complicity with the evil, while it shows that to many of us
are applicable the words in which another close observer of
what is going on, has described us Evangelists as "*Specimens*
" *of Truth petrified, fossilised, powerless Ministers of uncon-*
" *verted, Evangelical, fashionable, self-indulgent, unwarned, un-*
" *saved Congregations.*"

And now, in offering to the Christian Laity, what I have
called my companion-Pamphlet to the former, I would be-
speak your forbearance while I use " great plainness of
" speech." For I am speaking " as unto my Children ;"
" Judge ye what I say."

I owe my salvation (under God) to the *Christian Laity.*
It was one of *yourselves,* who " first taught *my* feet to tread
" the Heavenly Road." It was one of *yourselves* whose holy
and separate life and conversation first attracted me to the
cross of Christ. It was one of *yourselves* who first led me in
Spirit and in Truth to the Throne of Grace, and taught me
to lay aside my Private Manuals of Prayer, and pour out

my heart to God "as the Spirit gave me utterance." A dear young man of God among *yourselves* (now in glory) was my first Christian bosom-friend and daily companion at the time of my "first love;" now nearly seven-and-thirty years ago. It is to the *Godly Laity* that I have especially been indebted for true and loving sympathy in times of trial and persecution "for righteousness' sake." To *yourselves* am I indebted for my soul's most precious "spiritual meat, and "spiritual drink." Oh yes; and I do bless God too, for the great good I have received through the *prayers* of the Godly-Laity. Many a time have I enjoyed such near access to God, and entrance into the Holiest by the Blood of Jesus, not only with some of the rich and noble, but among the poor and needy. Even "in *poorest huts*," kneeling upon the brick floor of one and another poor saint's humble and scantily-furnished cottage, have tears of joy filled my eyes while from his heart he has been speaking to the Lord for me in prayer. I have gone to him, though his minister, "cast down," and have left him lifted up; I have gone to him in darkness and desolation, and have left him full of light and joy, through the power of the Holy Ghost which *he* has asked for me. And then, if I have thus to praise the Lord for what I owe the Christian Laity, in my *conversion*, and "*instruction in righteousness;*" for the *bright light of* a "*holy* and *separate walk* and *Conversation;*" for *sweet* "*fellow-* "*ship* with *the Father* and with *His Son Jesus Christ;* and "for *true* and *ever-ready sympathy* and *comfort* under *trials* and "*persecutions;*" what do I not owe them for their *letters?* Some make light of letters, and well they may, judging by the contents of many that are written; but I can bear wit- ness to much, *very much* blessing to my own soul through the letters of the Godly Laity.

One word more before I quit the subject of my *personal*

experience of the *power* of the *Godly Laity* for *good*. Who, in these my later days on earth, are my chief helpers now in the work of the Lord? It is the *Christian Laity*. These are (under God) the chief comforters of my soul in times of need; and, in looking forward to the days that may remain, it is to *these* my heart most clings in the sweet assurance that I shall prove, even to the end, the unbought, undeserved, undying love of God's dear children, rich and poor, among the Christian Laity.

Now to the more immediate subject of my pamphlet.

If it be true that we Evangelical Clergymen have "prophesied falsely," and been slumbering and sleeping at our posts, have not too many of you who hear us "*loved to have it so*"? Have you not loved to hear smooth things? Words of "peace" when there was "*no* peace"? Have you not been too well content that the sermon should be to you as a soothing lullaby, that should lull you into composure of spirit? something mild and moderate? not ardent, not zealous, not stirring, and rousing, and awakening, and alarming; a sort of "lovely song" from "one that hath a "pleasant voice, and can play well upon an instrument," not a sermon which comes home (through grace) to the *conscience*, and "pierceth even to the dividing asunder of soul and spirit, and of "the joints and marrow, and discerning the thoughts and intents of the heart"?

Or, if the Lord has given you a minister who, like the Apostle, has been no man-pleaser, and who has "not "shunned to declare unto you all the counsel of God," have you not soon made him feel that you are not his friends, but that he has become your enemy because he has told you the truth? His preaching has crossed your pleasures—brought divisions into your families—let the light into your consciences—condemned you on account of some allowed sins; some *easily besetting* sin it may be—reproved you for not acting up to what you know to be *just*, and *right*, and *lovely*, and of *good report*—brought the terrors of God's law before you—a terrible judgment to come—the undying worm—the unquenchable fire—the weeping, and wailing, and gnashing of teeth in hell. Thus, while you have known enough to make you *miserable*, you have not known enough to make you *happy*. You have stopped short of a full surrender. You have gone to a certain point, and have felt that to have gone farther would have caused you to be called " saints " by your worldly friends, and for *this* you were not prepared. You had no mind for daily taking up your cross "to follow Christ." You would willingly *wear* crosses round your necks, but *refused the cross of suffering persecution, scorn*, and *contempt*, and the *hatred of the world*, for Christ's sake and the Gospel's. Oh, ye *triflers*, ye *triflers !* Put away your ornamental crosses from off your necks ; and let me beseech you, " *in Christ's stead, be ye reconciled to God !*" *Play* at Religion no longer ! *Be in earnest, Be in earnest ! Awake*, ye sleepers ; *Awake*, before the midnight cry is heard, and He who *once* came to *save*, shall come to take terrible vengeance on " *them that know not God*, and *obey " not the Gospel of His Son !* "

Do *you* suppose that if the Christian Laity had done their duty, the Devil could ever have planted his foot so firmly in the Church of England as he has? I believe *not*. Do you suppose that those " lying Prophets," who now infest so many of the pulpits of the Protestant Church of England, defying all laws, Divine and human, and flaunting their Popish harlotries or Rationalistic doctrines with impunity in the very faces of our Bishops, ever could have had a *legalised position* amongst us if the Christian Laity had done their duty? I believe *not*.

I bless God that while I thus speak, I know *well* that there are many good men and true amongst you, who "cry "aloud and spare not." Who feed souls which we do not feed, and who do the work of Evangelists, which too many amongst us, so called Evangelical Ministers, *do not!* But, as a rule, you who hear us preach what, in one of the letters from my Christian Brethren, is called "a diluted and mutilated Gospel," *love to have it so!*

As I have to propose to the Christian Laity what may be considered to be a *strong "remedy,"* it becomes me to show that the *"disease"* is such as to require it; and this I shall have no difficulty in doing.

Perhaps one of the worst symptoms of the disease or the most humiliating proofs of the wide-spread conspiracy "against the Lord and against His Anointed," is that lately reported in the public papers of a visit paid by certain of our Church Bishops to the Greek Archbishop, who lately came to this country.

The writer of the article, after describing the teaching of the Greek Church to be "the co-ordinate Authority of "Tradition with Scripture—the saving virtue of human "works—the worship of pictures and relics—prayer to the "saints—transubstantiation of the consecrated bread and "wine into the real body and blood of Christ, goes on to "say, there is something exceedingly humiliating in the "attitude thus assumed on the part of our own Church. ". . . . English Bishops and Divines come, almost "cap in hand, to this degenerate representative of the "Greek Church pleading for recognition and admission to "communion; while he, on his part, assumes the attitude "of an Apostle dealing with heretics." And all this passes before the eyes of Protestant England without producing, so far as I know, one word of solemn protest or of indignant remonstrance. "BE ASTONISHED, O HEAVENS, "AND GIVE EAR, O EARTH!"

Priestcraft has been the ruin, as I believe we shall see, of this Church and Nation.

> " When Nations are to perish in their sins,
> " 'Tis in the Church the leprosy begins;
> " The Priest, whose office is, with zeal sincere,
> " To watch the Fountain, and preserve it clear,
> " Carelessly nods, and sleeps upon the brink,
> " While others poison what the flock must drink ;
> " Or, waking at the call of lust alone,
> " Infuses lies and errors of his own.
> " His unsuspecting sheep believe it pure,
> " And, tainted by the very means of cure,
> " Catch from each other a contagious spot,
> " The foul fore-runner of a general rot.
> " Then Truth is hushed, that heresy may preach,
> " And all is trash that Reason cannot teach :
> " Then God's own image, on the soul impress'd,
> " Becomes a mockery and a standing jest;
> " And Faith, the root whence only can arise
> " The graces of a life that wins the skies,
> " Loses at once all value and esteem,
> " Pronounced by greybeards a pernicious dream ;
> " Then Ceremony leads her bigots forth,
> " Prepared to fight for shadows of no worth ;
> " While truths, on which eternal things depend,
> " Find not, or hardly find, a single friend.
> " As soldiers watch the signal of command,
> " They learn to bow, to sit, to kneel, to stand ;
> ' Happy to fill Religion's vacant place
> " With hollow form, and gesture, and grimace."

Who would not think that these words of the immortal Cowper were the words of one who is *now a looker on* at what is passing before our own eyes in the Church of England ?

That A CONSPIRACY is formed among members of that Church "against the Lord," *is most certain.* Appeals to the Law Courts have been made, and, as regards any real permanent results, have failed—nay, heresy has been legalised! Appeals to our Bishops have been made, and failed, or greater encouragement to the Ritualists has been the result. The well-meant efforts of the Godly Laity, who ventured to suppose it possible that they might even have been *commended and assisted* in their faithfulness to the Lord and to His Truth, have been flung back at them with all the coldness of official reserve, if not with ill-concealed irritation at what has been regarded as their *audacity.* They have been told that they should remember that some prefer a more ornate, florid and more musical service than others; and that the Church of England is so constituted as to embrace within it "men of all schools of thought;" an expression I never see used but to repudiate and to nauseate it. I should like to know where we read in God's Holy Word that the Christian Religion is wide enough to take in "men of all schools of thought." Thus, while the enemies of the truth of God have thus come off triumphant, and have been encouraged in "bringing in "damnable heresies." the humble servants of the Lord (and I have oftentimes stood *amazed* at their humility) have entirely failed in their good contentions for the Faith, and have only been snubbed for their pains. This dark conspiracy has its ramifications more or less throughout the whole of England. A new kind of Inquisition has of late years been set up which radiates from its Head-Centres through all our towns and villages. New honours are conferred upon its officers among the inferior clergy as so many sops or bribes, and these, alas! are only too eagerly swallowed and taken by even some of our *best* men! The *narcotic effect* of these sops is too manifest to need pointing out. "Truth is" thereby "hushed that Heresy may "preach!" Large gatherings of the clergy are promoted, at which it is the fashion *for men of all parties* in the Church to assemble themselves together in Congresses, Conferences, Chapters, Clerical Meetings, &c. And even our *Evangelical Leaders* are not heard to say "Unto their assemblies mine "honour be not thou united."

At those highly-relished harvest thanksgivings some attraction is presented to *all*. There is "Holy Communion" in the morning, a jovial feast in the afternoon, and a merry dance at night; and, thus, while the Divine Life and Spiritual Light are *scarcely tolerated*, or only when *hidden* and *kept under*, Ritualism and Rationalism, and Worldliness, are rampant all around, and the people too generally "love to "have it so."

Scarcely was the ink dry in the last sentence I have written, when, taking up the *Record* of the 4th of April instant, I read in the leading article as follows:—"The "duty of administering the law lies upon THE BISHOPS; and "however unfaithful they may be to their obligations, they are "answerable before God, and will be strictly weighed in the "historical judgment of the future. The nobility of mind "to recognize the obligations of their office and to act upon "them, has been, unhappily, absent. Had they placed them- "selves boldly at the head of the Protestant feeling of the "country, they would have secured the safety of the Church "of England, and perhaps have averted changes of which "the ominous signs are to be seen in the future."

To all this I solemnly set my "Amen," and *more* than this, I believe that Englishmen are taxed to the extent of hundreds of thousands of pounds every year *for the propa-gation in the National Church of the most deadly and soul-*

destroying errors under the name of Protestant truth, and *for a very wide-spread suppression of the Gospel of God!*

This may be denied, but cannot be disproved; and, knowing this to be so, what are we to do? I answer in the first place, "CEASE YE FROM MAN." "Men of low "degree are vanity, and men of high degree are a lie; to be "laid in the balance they are altogether lighter than vanity." "Put not your trust in princes, nor in *any* child of man, "for there is *no* help in them." "Cease ye from man, for "wherein is he to be accounted of."

There *was* a time, which I well remember, when our rulers in Church and State might have stamped out this God-dishonouring Ritualism by one honest blow, as it lay impotent at their feet, in its first kindlings, thirty years ago. But now this monster evil, like a raging fire, defies all human effort, while it paralyses the very senses of the men who have so cruelly and wickedly tampered with it, if they have not willingly added fuel to the flames!

I say these men have lost their opportunity; and now, as the incendiary who has fired the building stands staring vacantly at the vastness of the conflagration which *he* has kindled, so do they now stand looking on in mute astonishment at the sight of a falling National Church, which, rescued out of the horrors of Popery by the blood of our martyred forefathers, has been, in an evil hour, committed by this great nation to their keeping.

It is a blessing, especially in times of "*overturning*" and "*confusion*" such as these, to find ourselves *shut up* to a particular course of action; and this one thing is certain, that God's people are *shut up unto the Lord.* "Of ourselves "we can do *nothing*." Hence, I do not, as some do, advocate Public Meetings. I dissent wholly from the words of good man who lately said, "Unhappily, at present, it is "only by public meetings that the Laity, as part of the "Church, can make its voice heard." The case were *indeed* hopeless if this were so. No; the hope of the godly is *not* in public meetings.

Some advocate an extension of the "Episcopate." This *I* dare not do. Chosen as our Bishops now are by the Prime Minister of the day, I might thereby be fostering and increasing the very evils of which I complain, and against which I am recording my solemn protest. An extension of the Episcopate may mean also (as sad experience daily shows) a concurrent extension of Popery, Infidelity, Ritualism, and Rationalism, and a corresponding suppression of the truth of the Gospel. No; rather than any *increase*, I would advocate a considerable *decrease* of the Episcopate.

Memorials to our rulers in Church and State are so much waste paper; while Convocation I regard as a *great sham*. And I am deeply grieved, in faithfulness, to be obliged to add that *even the long-loved and long-acknowledged Leaders of our Evangelical Body are nowhere, when most of all their presence is required at " the front."*

Well, then, "CEASE YE FROM MAN"! And what next are we to do? I answer, GATHER ROUND THE LORD IN UNITED SERVICE REGARDLESS OF NON-ESSENTIAL DIFFERENCES AND DENOMINATIONAL DISTINCTIONS.

Away with every human barrier that separates the saints from the Lord, and from each other. ABOVE ALL LET LAY PREACHING OF THE GOSPEL BE INTRODUCED INTO THE CHURCH OF ENGLAND AS QUICKLY AND AS EXTENSIVELY AS POSSIBLE, as Mr. Cowper Temple so wisely proposed in Parliament.

It was only the other day that one of our Bishops, being

appealed to against the Popish doctrines and doings of a Ritualistic Clergyman, recommended his memorialists to go home and try what a mutual *compromise* and *concession* on both sides would do towards making peace in the parish.

What! *compromise* between believers and unbelievers! between righteousness and unrighteousness! between light and darkness! between Christ and Belial! between the Temple of God and idols! Is it come to *this?* Ah, beloved, HEREIN IS OUR WEAKNESS! *Hence*, the afflictions and in-flictions wherewith we are on all sides now beset! *Compro-mise* between the *friends* and *enemies* of *the Truth of God!* We are *betrayed*, we are *betrayed!* and that *from within;* and hence the days of the Established Church are numbered. Good men and true might, at one time, have purged her from her blots and disfigurements, but such men were not found, and Diocese after Diocese, and Parish after Parish, and Pulpit after Pulpit, have been thrown open to the enemy, until God's dear people have been starved out, and the world, for which Christ emphatically says, "*I pray not*," runs riot in the Churches of England in their room! *Compromise* between *true Evangelists* and *Ritualists*? *God forbid!* Alas! that the day ever should have come when peace at any price should be thus counselled to us inferior Clergy by Episcopal lips! andthe law of England's highest Court quoted in justifica-tion of such timid counsels! I, for one, had rather far have been advised by my Spiritual superior to go back to my parish, torn and distracted as it might have been by this accursed Ritualism, and there earnestly to contend "for the "faith once delivered unto the saints," and to give place, *no, not for an hour*, to the enemies of the Gospel; and if my Spiritual Father had pleaded that the Privy Council is one of " *the powers that be*," and that " whosoever resisteth the "power, resisteth the ordinance of God," I would then humbly have reminded him that there is another Scripture in which the Spirit teaches me to "*obey God rather than man*," and that whereinsoever man requires of me that which God forbids, I must, at all hazards and regardless of all consequences, "*render unto God the things that are God's.*"

It is this miserable policy of *compromise* and *concession* that has landed us where we are. The glorious Reformation which made England's greatness, never *could* have been accomplished had our Reformers consented to a *compromise*. As "*No peace with Rome*" was *their* war-cry, so "*No peace with Ritualism and Rationalism*" must be *ours*. And while the "enemies of the Cross of Christ" are madly set upon betraying Him, so must we who, through grace, "glory" *only* in that Cross, be determined, in God's strength, that we will not have it so.

But to this end we must be *united in action*. In union is strength, and none knows this better than the devil, and therefore he seeks to divide us. We must not regard *non essential* differences. There ever will be these while the world lasts. Unity is not uniformity. "Grace be with all "them that love our Lord Jesus Christ in sincerity" was the Apostle's rule; and no faithful follower of the Lord has any right or need to *add to* or *diminish* it. I believe that I, so doing you would do this three-fold good. First, you would stop the clamours of a great multitude for the dis-establishment of the National Church; secondly, by bringing such a flood of light into the Establishment you would wake up us slumbering Evangelicals, and provoke us to more faithful and self-denying labours; and, lastly, you would either see these unfortunate men, the Ritualists and Rationalists, cast away their idols "to the moles and to "the bats" and follow Jesus, or driven away from before the power of truth into the dark and dismal regions of that great apostasy whose soul-destroying work they are now doing under the mask and garb of Protestantism.

A General Election is close at hand. Let every Christian voter lose sight of every other requirement in the candidate for his vote in comparison with his determination to support measures that are directly framed to promote THE FULL AND FREE ADMISSION OF THE CHRISTIAN LAITY INTO EVERY DEPARTMENT OF OUR PAROCHIAL MINISTRATIONS IN WHICH THEY CAN BE SCRIPTURALLY AND LAWFULLY OCCUPIED, in the exercise of whatever gifts God may have given them. "A gift from God is "*virtually a command,* "given to every one to profit withal;" of course to profit *others.*

Pass a law whereby Parishioners may have the use of their Parish Churches for the worship and service of Almighty God, and for speaking in the Name of the Lord, instead of their being almost always closed against them as at present, except at the will of the Incumbent. Let *Lay Evangelists* do *in* our Parish Churches and Chapels what they now do *out* of them, viz. : *seek to save sinners by preaching the Word.* I believe there would be no lack of good and faithful men qualified by the Holy Ghost for the work, even though they never may have learned a line of Greek or Latin. *Awakened Hearers must* have *awakened Preachers*—men in *advance of themselves* in "the "knowledge of the truth." Unawakened men are *in the way,* and ought to be removed out of it, as hinderers of the Gospel, and to make room for *enlightened and living men.* Or, if preach they *must,* let them be restricted to certain times and seasons when they will find, if I mistake not, that they will preach to sleepers like themselves.

I pause for a moment to give time to some who may read this Pamphlet to recover their breath ! * * * * * *

And now let me repeat my solemn conviction that NOTHING HALF SO GOOD COULD BE DEVISED FOR THE PRESENT FEARFUL CRISIS AS THIS. I would go further—I would open our Parish Churches and Pulpits to ministers of *Non-Conforming and Presbyterian Churches*, and have the Evangelical Clergy in like manner preach the Gospel *any and everywhere, according to the command of the Lord ;* lovingly interchanging places of worship with our Non-Conforming brethren and Presbyterians, without regard to any human denominations or distinctions whatever. Let all of us Evangelists be henceforward *associated* in "working the "work of God," in brotherly love, like the first Disciples of the Lord.

The truth is that the law of the land stands in the way of the Gospel of Christ, and so in the way of the salvation of poor lost sinners from death and hell, and of the building up of the Church of God "in their most holy faith ;" *and it ought not to be allowed to do so any longer.*

Some may be ready to say to me, "Ah, you would not "have said what you now say before you had resigned your "Vicarage with your comfortable home, your Glebe, your "Tithes, your Fees, your Offerings, and your Autocratic "power." I believe I *should*, if I had seen so *fearful* a state of things as now I see *everywhere around me.*

I am perfectly certain that the time has come when the old régime should be broken up, and when that dreadful word "*routine*" should be, *from first to last, inapplicable to the preaching of the everlasting Gospel.* What we now want is this :—*Heaven-called, Heaven-taught, Heaven-sent,* and *Heaven-blessed Lay Evangelists in thousands ;* and the time has fully come when Englishmen ought to *insist* on legislation for her many millions of people who are now "*perishing* "*for lack of knowledge.*" Yes, I hope soon to see the day *when Godly Lay Evangelists shall come in amongst us by thousands*, and by the light of *Truth*, and of a holy self-denying life, "put to silence the "ignorance of "foolish men."

I *quite* believe that there is a noble army of truly Godly Laity, Divinely furnished and equipped, only waiting the word to re-inforce us from all orders and ranks; from the converted nobility and gentry down to the poorest artisans and labouring men. Yes, I believe that Godly Laymen are *burning with an ardent longing for the work of evangelization;* and I am quite certain that we have nothing to fear from letting them in, but *everything to hope.* You would not find the Godly Laity turning our beautiful Churches into Popish Mass Houses. You would not find *them* intoning the prayers, nor preaching in a surplice, nor chanting the Psalms, nor swinging the incense-pot, nor bowing to the "altar," nor turning their backs upon the people, nor elevating the paten, nor turning to the east, nor kissing a stole, nor enticing young maidens to come and confess their sins unto them before early "matins" or after late "even-song," and to receive absolution from *themselves.* No: the Godly Lay-Evangelists would show unto us "a more excellent way." And you would not find *them* preaching that soul-destroying doctrine, *Baptismal Regeneration*, nor Rationalistic Doctrines, nor the *opus operatum* of Confirmation through laying on of hands, and salvation by works, and transubstantiation of bread and wine into the actual Body and Blood of the Lord, and prayers *to* the dead, and prayers *for* the dead, and the worship of Mary, and the unlawfulness of evening communions, and such like; but you would find them *then* what you find them *now*, ready at all times to serve the Lord and His Church and people faithfully, according to the gifts given to them of God.

No doubt if the day should happily come (and I believe it *will* come, and that we may see it) when we Evangelical Clergymen shall be *largely re-inforced* by " *the foolish things*," and " *the weak things*," and " *the base things of the world*," and " *things which are despised*," yea, and " *things which are not*," which " God hath chosen to bring to nought things that are," there will be a *wonderful* change ; a *marvellous* revival in place of that darkness and death which now prevail *to an alarming extent*.

But *begin at once*, ye Godly Laity. You are (under God) *of yourselves* A " POWER." I want you *prayerfully and solemnly to consider this.* You have too long tamely *delegated* that power to us Ministers ; but in so doing you have, I believe, displeased the Lord. You must not think that your responsibility ceases when you have got up an indignation-meeting, and obtained signatures to a memorial. No : while you stand looking one at another, wondering what will come next,—one man afraid to act with vigour and promptness because he fears he shall offend *somebody*, and another because he is afraid he may displease *somebody else*,—the enemy is gaining ground upon us ! Though *we* slumber and sleep, *they* do not.

Set to work *at once, and in real earnest, I beseech you.* I shall gladly receive any words of counsel or of sympathy in the work which I am endeavouring to do for God and for souls, from my brothers and sisters of the Godly Laity or Clergy who may be inclined to offer them.

Of course I expect to be considered a mere Visionary and Enthusiast, or even " *beside myself*," by the children of this world, for proposing to let in upon our hitherto sacred inclosures the flood of the Godly Laity. But I believe that, humanly speaking, nothing *half* so good could be done; and that I use the words of soberness and truth when I say that it will, by God's blessing, *be the saving of all that is most valuable to England, and which, at this moment, is being wrested from her by her own sons.*

Some may think that the Godly Laity would make a bad use of our Churches were they to be thrown open to them by Law, as I propose. *So bad* a use of them, think you, as is *now* made by the *Ritualists?* And that Lay-Evangelists would preach unsound doctrines from our pulpits. *So unsound*, think you, as those now preached by the *Ritualists?* and, alas! *not by Ritualists only.* At all events, let us (looking to the Lord) *try the experiment at once.* Let us not tarry for the slow process of the law. Let *us* who are ordained of God to the ministry, open our hearts and Parishes and take in AT ONCE those blessed Laymen upon whom we have been looking down with something like *contempt* or *Pharisaic pride.* Let *us* be *forward* to hold out to them the right hand of fellowship. Let us deem it our *honour* and our *privilege* to have them henceforth *fighting, side by side with us, the "good fight of faith."*

I remember that it is to the godly Laity we owe it that we can now assemble ourselves together for hearing the Word and for worship in any number we will, "no man "making us afraid." Thanks be to that blessed man of God, the foremost among England's nobles, none can now lawfully break in upon our religious assemblies to count heads, and if he should find there so many as twenty, to summon their leader before a court of justice to answer for a breach of the laws of Christian England! Oh! I love to think of that *true* specimen of a noble Soldier of the Cross standing like a rock in the House of Lords determined, by God's help, to scatter to the winds that wicked edict that no private assembly of Christians should exceed nineteen in number; and though the opposition he encountered *(shame, shame upon us !)* came *chiefly* from the Bench of Bishops, he nevertheless accomplished his God-like work. All honour to *him*, and TO GOD ALL PRAISE !

Ye Christian WOMEN of England, of *you* the Lord hath need in this solemn crisis ! Your power for good or evil is *great !* Your influence *for* Christ's cause or *against* it is *great !* Arise, and be ye to us " as corner stones, polished after the "similitude of a palace." " Be ye not conformed to this "world." I will, "saith the Lord, that women adorn them- "selves in *modest apparel* with shamefacedness and sobriety." For *example's sake* too, before your *children* and *servants* let your " adorning not be that outward adorning of plaiting "the hair, and of wearing of gold, and of putting on of "apparel ; but let it be the hidden man of the heart, in "that which is not corruptible, even the ornament of a "meek and quiet spirit, which is in the sight of God of "great price."

Beware ye professing Christian women of that *crying sin, the love of dress !* that *parent sin,* as I may call it, by which immorality is encouraged in either sex !

A Christian lady writing to me recently, says, " I "long to see my own sex as real salt in society." Come, then, ye *godly* women and "labour with us much in the "Lord." *Wondrous blessing* God *has* given, *is* giving, and yet *will* give to your work done by faith in Jesus.

And now let me, in conclusion, ask my readers to imagine how confirmatory of what I have written were the following words in a letter I received from Ireland just as I had come to the end of my " Thoughts for the Christian Laity." The writer, who is a truly devoted servant of the Lord, and

who mourns over what he calls "the Apostasy of Christen-
"dom," says, in speaking of my Pamphlet to the Evangelical Clergy, "I do not expect it will influence *many*
"of the clergy. Your efforts will be more successfully
"employed with Christian Laymen, among whom you
"will find a goodly number ready to sympathise with you.
"UTILISE THE LAY POWER"—the *one thought upper-
most in my mind, and in my prayers, all the while I have
been writing this Pamphlet!* I felt for the moment
as if I were *in the very presence of God.* It seemed to
me *as though the Lord had said to me, audibly,* "UTILISE
THE LAY POWER." Such, at all events, do I believe to be
according to the Lord's mind, and to *Him* do I, with *deepest
reverence,* commend these "Thoughts for the Christian
Laity." If I rightly discern the signs of the times,
the days are gone in which we Clergymen can safely
stand up for the rigid conservancy of all our rights.
A most ominous vote has just been given in the House
of Commons upon the debate of the Bill entitled, "The
Burials Bill," which, if it becomes law, will throw open
our Parish Churchyards to our Non-Conforming brethren,
and in this I read another *cogent* reason why we should *at
once heartily encourage Lay Agency to the uttermost.* If we
are to see our brother officiating lawfully in our Parochial
Churchyards *outside,* why should we not hold up our hands
for his admission *inside* our Churches? Why pass a law that
is to give him authority to bury the *bodies* of the *dead,* and
yet continue to frown upon his work of helping to save the
souls of the *living?*

In conclusion, it is *on the authority of the word of God
that I give this counsel.* We are told therein that when the
Spirit of God came upon the seventy elders in the camp of
Israel they prophesied and ceased not. And there ran a

young man and told Moses that some "did prophesy in the
"camp. And Joshua, Moses' servant, said, my lord Moses,
"forbid them. And Moses said unto him, Enviest thou for
"my sake? WOULD GOD THAT ALL THE LORD'S PEOPLE
"WERE PROPHETS, AND THAT THE LORD WOULD PUT HIS
"SPIRIT UPON THEM."

In like manner, when there was great persecution against
the Church at Jerusalem, THE DISCIPLES WERE ALL SCAT-
TERED "ABROAD, AND WENT EVERYWHERE PREACHING THE
"WORD. And the hand of the Lord was with them, and a
"great number believed and turned to the Lord. And when
"tidings of these things came unto the ears of the church
"which was in Jerusalem, they sent forth Barnabas that he
"should go as far as Antioch, who, when he came and had
"seen the grace of God, was glad; and exhorted them that
"with purpose of heart they would cleave unto the Lord;
"for he was a good man and full of the Holy Ghost and of
"Faith. And much people were added unto the Lord."

Thus the wrath of those who persecuted the Preachers of
the Gospel in the days of the Apostles was made to praise
the Lord; and they that would have suppressed the Truth
as it is in Jesus were the unintentional causes of its wider
proclamation and its greater success.

And this is what I pray God we may soon see in England.
CHRIST'S TRUE DISCIPLES GOING EVERYWHERE HAND IN
HAND WITH US MINISTERS OF THE GOSPEL, PREACHING
AND TEACHING THE GLAD TIDINGS OF REDEMPTION. And
then, though some should "preach Christ of envy and
"strife, and some also of good will," all true Christians will
join with the Apostle Paul, when he says, "Notwithstand-
"ing every way, whether in pretence or in Truth, CHRIST
"IS PREACHED; and I therein *do* rejoice, and *will*
"rejoice."

As we none of us know which word we speak or write may be our *last*, I would here assure my dear Brethren in the Ministry and among the Christian Laity, that the only *real* regret I feel at having thus ventured to raise my voice, amongst others, at the present *awful crisis*, is the knowledge that I have thereby given offence, though (God is witness) *most* unintentionally, to many of them. My Pamphlets have cost me the loss of some of my oldest and dearest Brethren and Friends, even of thirty or forty years standing. And yet, while feeling *most deeply* the trial which any man not altogether devoid of good feeling *must* suffer under such a loss, I cannot say, in the midst of all, that I would wish or hardly dare to retract a single line that I have written.

Printed by W. H. & L. COLLINGRIDGE, 117 to 120, Aldersgate Street, London.

www.ingramcontent.com/pod-product-compliance
Lightning Source LLC
Chambersburg PA
CBHW081308040426
42452CB00014B/2708